It be-h●●ves me to dedicate this book to:

_____

HOLY COW,
I SURE DO LOVE YOU!

AMY KROUSE ROSENTHAL
TOM LICHTENHELD

Abrams Image, New York

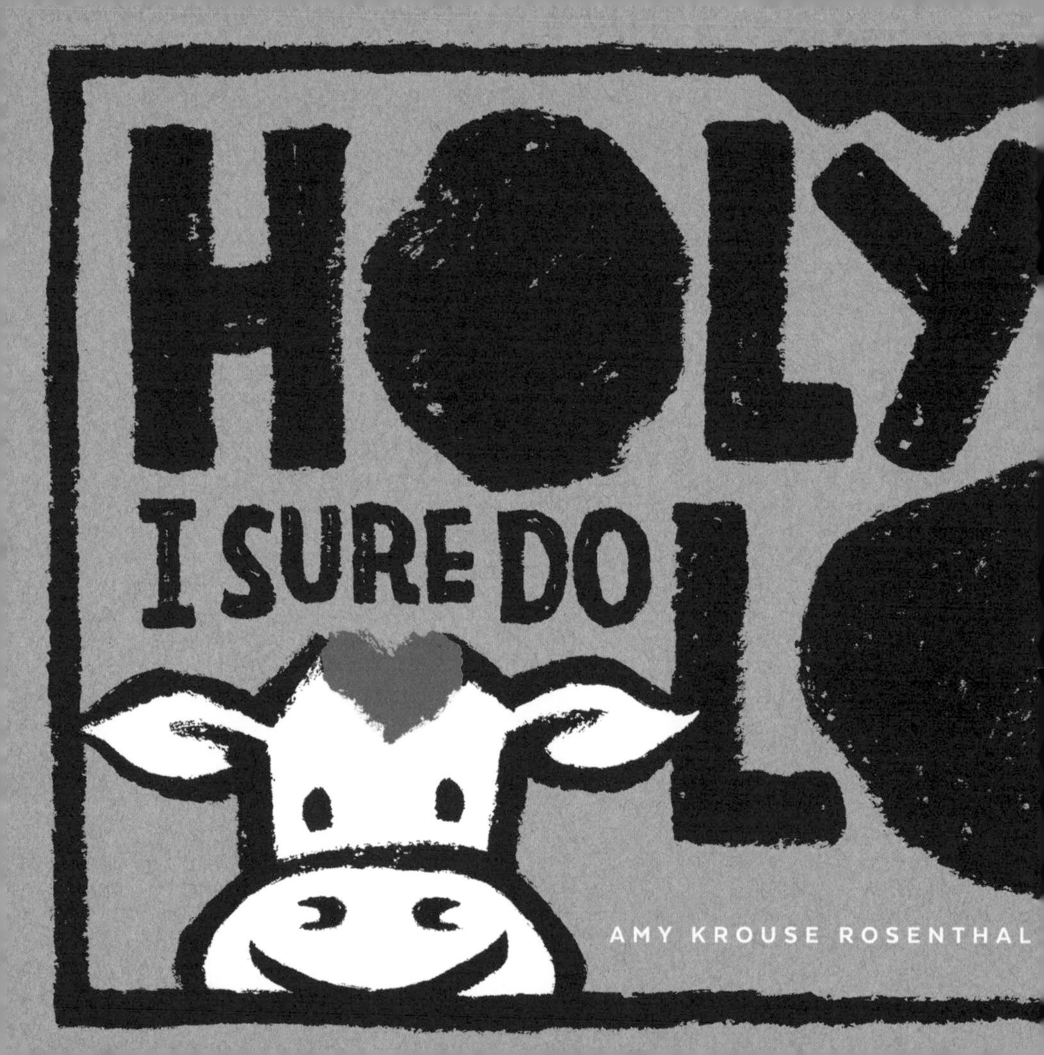
HOLY
I SURE DO
AMY KROUSE ROSENTHAL

COW, LOVE YOU

A little book that's oddly moo-ving

TOM LICHTENHELD

Moo-ooh baby, I sure do love you.

I love you every

Good m●●-d ...

which way . . .

Bad m●●-d . . .

I love you in every language.

Ti a-m●●, amore mio.

M●●-la-la,
je t'aime.

I'm always happy to see you.

And I'm sad when you leave.

Well ...

Words can't fully express how I feel.

Good thing there are e-m●●-jis.

(Of course, I also love pizza, but that's a m●●-t point.)

You fill my life with song ...

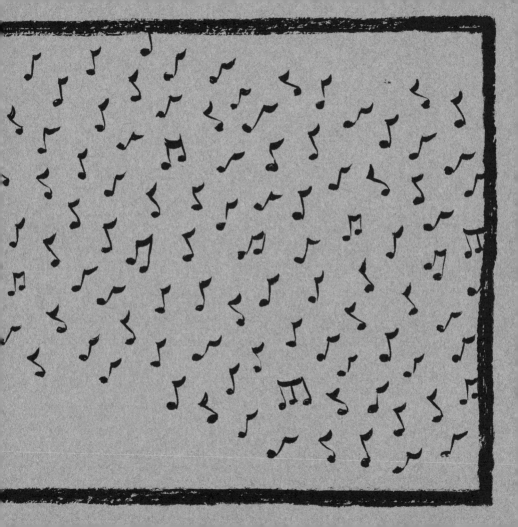

You help me through the rough patches.

Then it's sm●●-th sailing.

My love for yo

My love for you is as big as ...

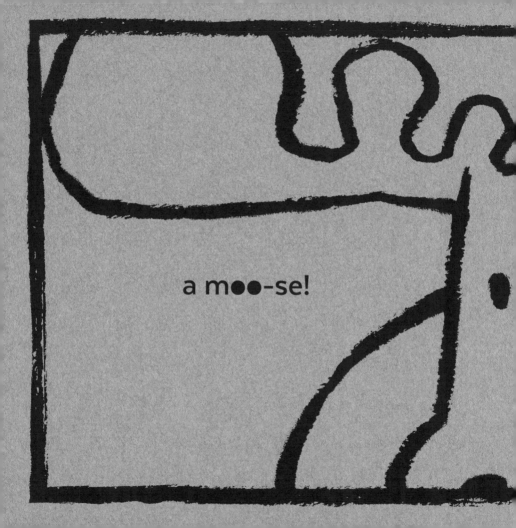

a m●●-se!

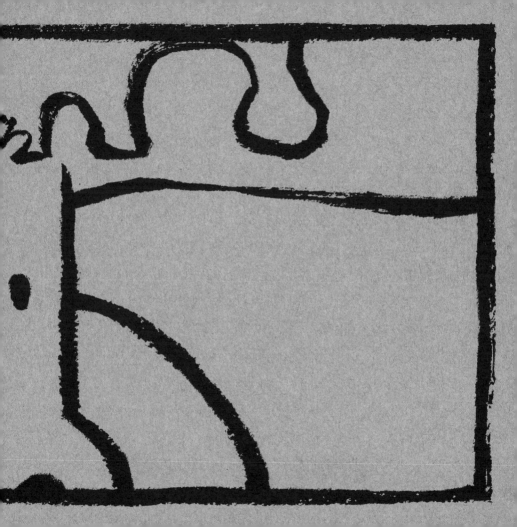

Your love is a treasure ...

You make my heart soar.

HOLY DO I LOVE

COW, EVER YOU!

And I couldn't possibly love you ...

m●●-er.
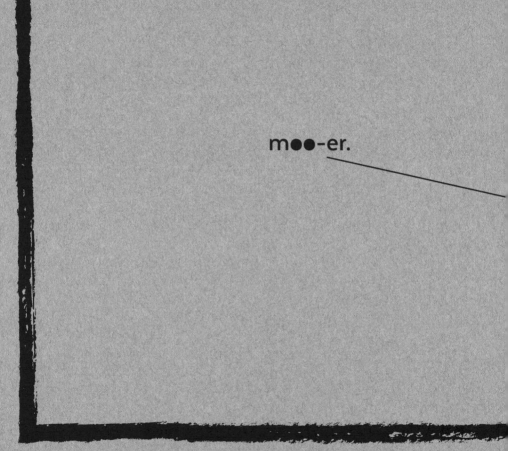

Editor: Karrie Witkin
Production Manager: Kathleen Gaffney
Design Manager: Devin Grosz

ISBN: 978-1-4197-2217-2

Text copyright © 2016 Amy Krouse Rosenthal
Illustrations copyright © 2016 Tom Lichtenheld

Printed and bound in China
10 9 8 7 6 5 4 3 2

Abrams Image books are available at special discounts when purchased in quantity for premiums and promotions as well as fundraising or educational use. Special editions can also be created to specification. For details, contact specialsales@abramsbooks.com or the address below.

ABRAMS
The Art of Books

195 Broadway
New York, NY 10007
abramsbooks.com